G is for Galaxy

An Out of This World Alphabet

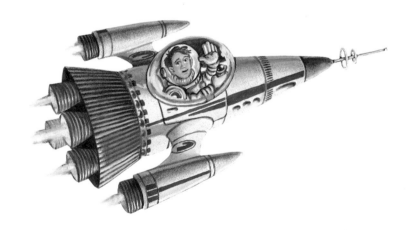

Written by Janis Campbell & Cathy Collison and Illustrated by Alan Stacy

A special thank you to the super stars at Michigan State University's Abrams Planetarium—David Batch, Shane Horvatin, and John French —for being our first readers and giving us great advice.

—Janis and Cathy

Text Copyright © 2005 Janis Campbell and Cathy Collison
Illustration Copyright © 2005 Alan Stacy

Sleeping Bear Press™

315 E. Eisenhower Parkway, Suite 200
Ann Arbor, MI 48108
www.sleepingbearpress.com

Sleeping Bear Press is an imprint of Gale, a part of Cengage Learning.

Printed and bound in the United States.

10 9 8 7 6 5 4 3 2 (pbk)
10 9 8 7 6 5 4 3 2 (case)

Library of Congress Cataloging-in-Publication Data

Collison, Catherine.
G is for galaxy : an out of this world alphabet / by Cathy Collison and Janis Campbell ; illustrated by Alan Stacy.
p. cm.
Summary: "This A to Z children's pictorial covers topics such as the planets, craters, comets, orbits, and telescopes. Each word related to our galaxy or to space is introduced with a simple poem for younger readers and also includes detailed expository text for older readers"—Provided by publisher.

pbk   ISBN 13: 978-1-58536-335-3   **case**   ISBN 13: 978-1-58536-255-4
      ISBN 10: 1-58536-335-9   ISBN 10: 1-58536-255-7

1. Astronomy—Dictionaries, Juvenile. 2. Astronomy—Pictorial works— Juvenile literature. I. Campbell, Janis (Janis M.) II. Stacy, Alan, ill. III. Title.
QB46.C743 2005
520'.3—dc22   2005006023

For Andrew, Colin, and Steve—
the brightest stars in my universe.

JANIS

For Dad, who always taught me to shine.
And for my other stars: Bill, Maggie, and Robert.

CATHY

For Dad, who had his part in making the dream of space
exploration a reality; for both of my parents, who gave me a sense
of imagination and a wonder about life and all creation.

Deo gratia

ALAN

A is for Astronomy,
        the science of outer space.
    It's how we explore the nighttime sky,
        and keep track of each planet's place.

Astronomy is the study of space—including the stars, planets, and galaxies. It's a science both old and new. Even today, astronomers are always making new discoveries. Maybe you'll want to be one, too.

A is for astronauts. Think of them as sailors in space. The word comes from the Greek language. *Astron* means star and *nautes* means sailor. America's astronaut program got its start in the late 1950s and early '60s. Alan B. Shepard became the first American in space on May 5, 1961, shortly after a Russian cosmonaut (the word the Russians use for astronaut) had orbited the Earth on April 12, 1961. John Glenn became the first American to orbit the Earth on February 20, 1962.

A is also for asteroids. They are giant rocks in space, almost acting like very tiny planets. They orbit the sun in a path, which runs mainly between Mars and Jupiter.

Big bang! Is that a noise? No, big bang is the name of a big idea—a theory that explains how the universe began. Many scientists believe that the universe began with a huge explosion about 13 billion or more years ago. This explosion, or bang, led to the creation of the building blocks of the universe, which began forming our galaxies. Even though this happened billions of years ago, astronomers think the effect is still happening today as our universe continues to grow.

B is also for black holes. Imagine a big black invisible space, like a dark hole. That's what scientists believe happens when a large star explodes or dies, leaving a huge amount of gravity. Black holes sound mysterious and they are. Scientists hope to find out more about them.

B is for the Big Bang;
no, not a crashing sound,
but the beginning of the universe,
according to what scientists have found.

C is for Crater,
deep and sometimes round.
The huge hole is a sure sign
that a meteorite once hit the ground.

On Earth you can find craters, large holes left when a meteoroid, or large rock from space, smashes down into the Earth. If this meteoroid doesn't burn up before hitting the ground, then it's called a meteorite. Other planets and moons also have craters. One of the best-known craters in the United States is near Winslow, Arizona. The word crater comes from the Greek language. The Greek word, *krater*, means bowl.

D is the Dinosaurs,
    the giant creatures who made Earth home.
But when a mighty comet struck,
    they would no longer roam.

The disappearance of the dinosaurs is a bit of a mystery. What caused this to happen? One idea is that a huge meteorite hit the Earth. Many scientists believe that a comet or asteroid hit our planet 65 million years ago with so much force that it was like a gigantic bomb exploding, causing huge destruction. It may have set off earthquakes, tidal waves, and caused big clouds of dust and debris. These dusty clouds may have blocked the sun and brought darkness and cold for months on end. That drastic change in the climate meant the dinosaurs could not survive, although other living creatures could.

D is also for dogs in space. Two dogs survived a trip to outer space in 1960 when Belka and Strelka orbited the Earth in the Soviet Union's spacecraft. Later, President Kennedy was given a puppy of Strelka's as a gift.

Dd

E is for Earth.
Our planet's so much fun.
Luckily for us, we're the right
distance from the sun.

Home, sweet home. The Earth is our home and it sure is one sweet planet. In fact, Earth is the only place in our galaxy that we know of that can support human life. All of the planets except Earth are named after gods or goddesses. The name Earth comes from an old English word, meaning base or ground. Earth is the third planet from the sun. We have the right atmosphere for life with plenty of oxygen and plenty of water. The Earth orbits at a tilt like a spinning top. Each day is 24 hours long and it takes about 365 days for the Earth to orbit the sun.

E is also for Earth Day. Our environment is special, and people want to make sure we keep treating it with care. So every year we celebrate and look for new ways to take care of our planet on April 22.

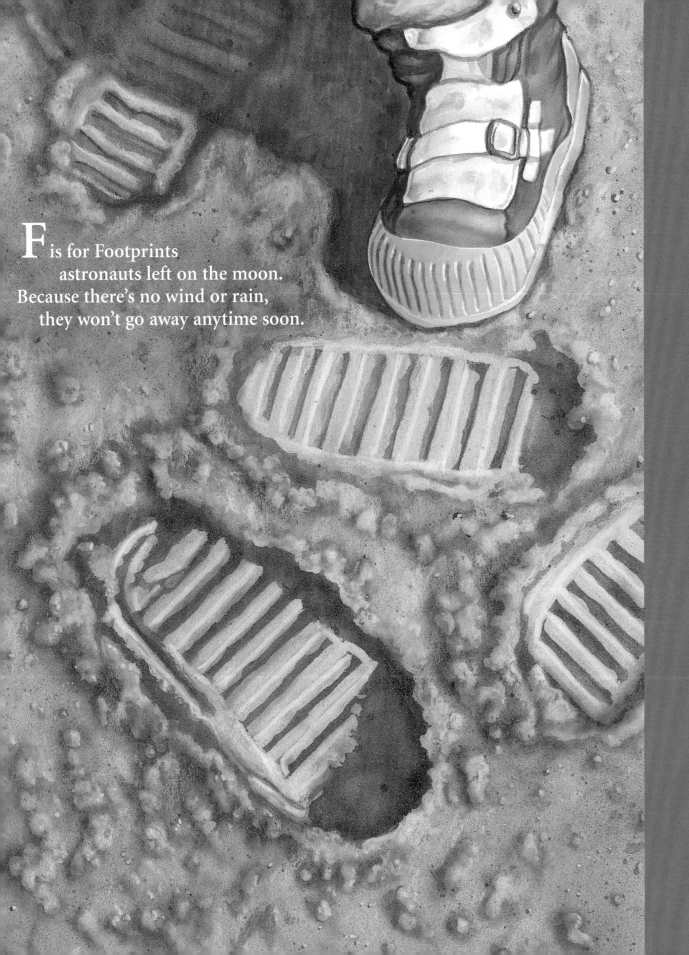

F is for Footprints
astronauts left on the moon.
Because there's no wind or rain,
they won't go away anytime soon.

Footprints in the sand or the snow on Earth don't last very long. But did you know there are footprints on the moon that will last for thousands of years? The footprints are from the astronauts who have walked on the moon. On July 20, 1969, American astronaut Neil Armstrong made the first human footprint on the moon. Neil's words are still famous. He said, "That's one small step for man, one giant leap for mankind." Besides footprints, Neil and astronaut Buzz Aldrin left an American flag and a plaque on the moon. Also on that famous mission, called *Apollo 11*, was astronaut Michael Collins. The message on the plaque says, "We came in peace for all mankind."

Ff

G
g

A galaxy is a family of stars, but in such a huge family you'd never meet every member. There are billions of stars in one galaxy. Planets are part of a galaxy, too. So are dust and gases. Gravity keeps the family together. We are in the Milky Way galaxy. It is a huge galaxy of about 100 billion stars, but astronomers remind us that the Milky Way is just one galaxy out of billions. Galaxies come in different shapes and sizes. Our galaxy has been compared to a big pinwheel.

G is for Galaxy,
a big family of stars so bright.
Ours is called the Milky Way,
a small part we see each night.

H h

H is for Halley.
Hip, hip hooray!
He predicted a comet's return
so it's named after him today.

Astronomer Edmund Halley isn't the only one who thinks comets are cool. The comet is an icy ball revolving around the sun—with a tail of dust and gas. Comet followers call them dirty snowballs ever since an astronomer used that description in 1950. Or you could say a comet looks like a star with long, flowing hair trailing behind it. The Greeks saw comets like that and called them *aster kometes*, or hairy stars. People used to think these comets came at any time and sometimes were afraid of them, thinking the comet was a sign of some bad news.

Edmund Halley changed that thinking. The English astronomer was the first person to recognize that comets had an orbit too. Halley was so good at studying comets, he was able to predict when one comet would return. That comet is named after him. Halley's comet returns about every 76 years. It was last seen flying by in 1986 and will come again in about 2061. Does that sound like a long time? It is, but don't worry, there will be other comets you can catch flying by.

ISTIMIRANT STELLA

BAYEUX · TAPESTRY · 1066

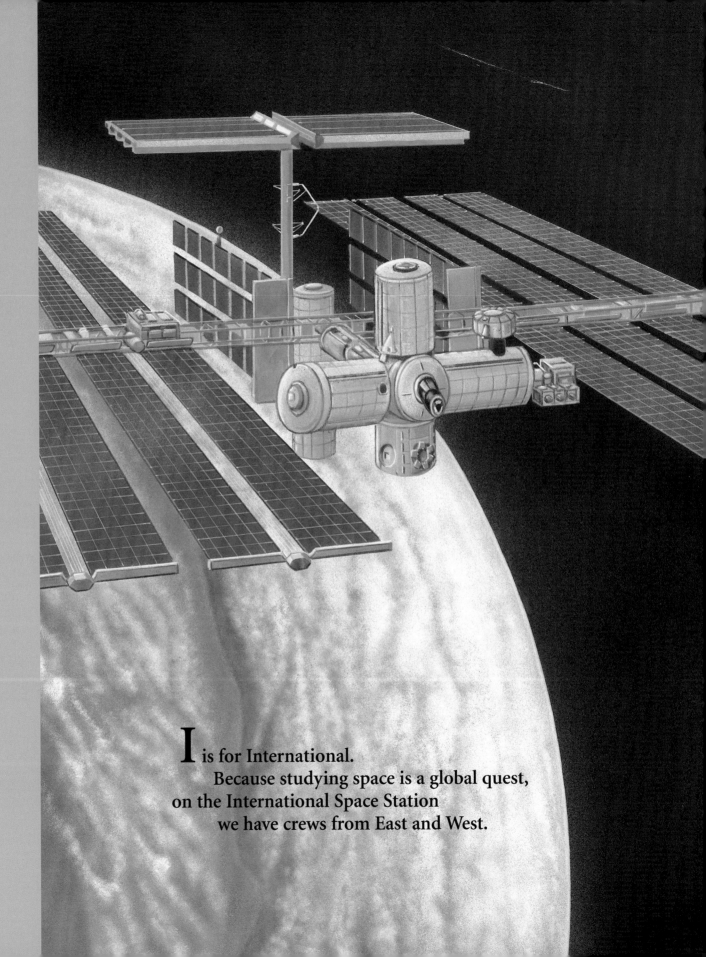

I is for the International Space Station. It is truly international with 16 countries helping to build and operate this laboratory in space. The space station has been up in orbit since 1998. The first crew arrived in 2000. The station is a place where space scientists can do experiments while continuing to work on building the giant space structure. The space station should be finished by 2010.

Imagine you might someday travel to outer space. What would you wear? What would you want to do there? Plenty of writers and moviemakers have used their imagination to show us a far-out vision of space. Moviemaker George Lucas imagined an amazing world in his *Star Wars* movies. *E.T.* was Steven Spielberg's movie using his imagination on what would happen if a friendly alien came to Earth. Let your imagination take off!

I is for International.
	Because studying space is a global quest,
on the International Space Station
		we have crews from East and West.

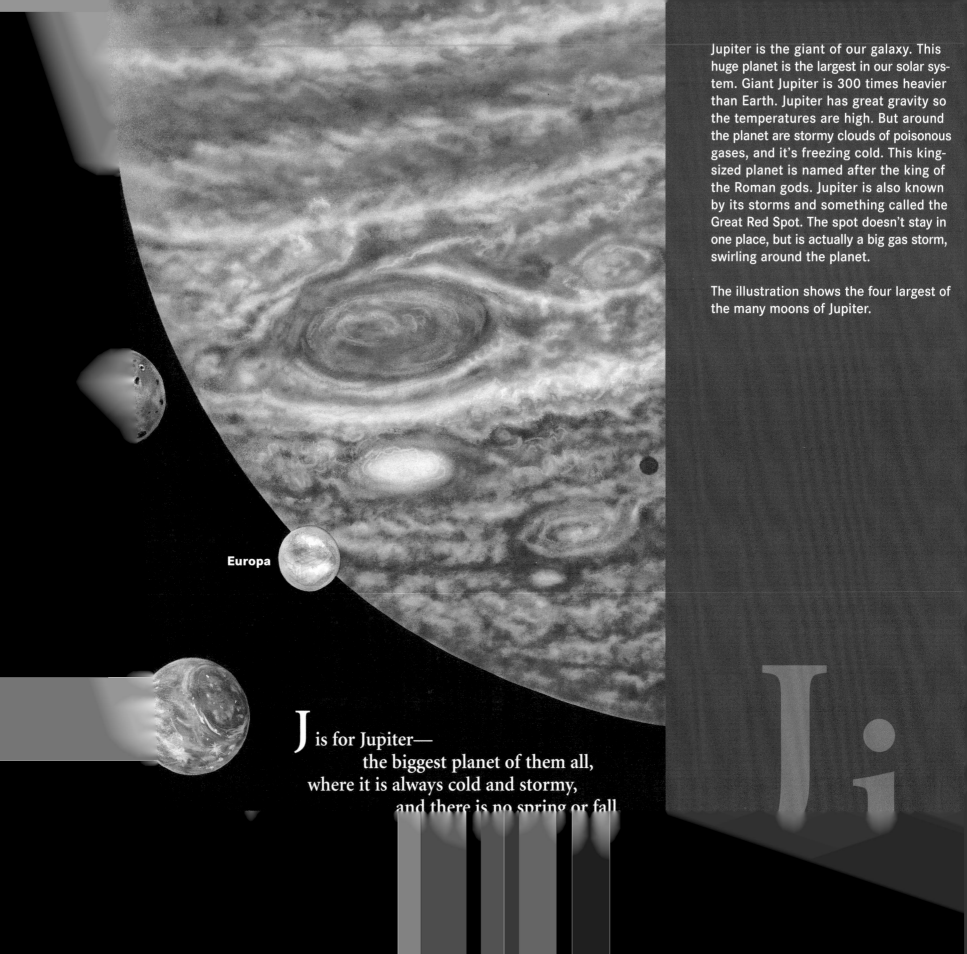

Jupiter is the giant of our galaxy. This huge planet is the largest in our solar system. Giant Jupiter is 300 times heavier than Earth. Jupiter has great gravity so the temperatures are high. But around the planet are stormy clouds of poisonous gases, and it's freezing cold. This king-sized planet is named after the king of the Roman gods. Jupiter is also known by its storms and something called the Great Red Spot. The spot doesn't stay in one place, but is actually a big gas storm, swirling around the planet.

The illustration shows the four largest of the many moons of Jupiter.

Europa

J is for Jupiter—
the biggest planet of them all,
where it is always cold and stormy,
and there is no spring or fall.

Jj

K is for Kennedy,
the president with a plan
for us to race to outer space
and find out all we can.

President John F. Kennedy is the leader given credit for pushing the United States forward in space exploration. When he became president, there was a race for exploring outer space. Russian cosmonaut Yury Gagarin was the first person in space and first person to orbit the Earth. President Kennedy wanted the United States to be the first country to put a man on the moon. That goal was accomplished in July of 1969 when Neil Armstrong set foot on the moon. Today you can visit the Kennedy Space Center by Cape Canaveral, Florida. The center is named in honor of President Kennedy.

In 2004, President George W. Bush announced big new goals for America's space program, including building a new spacecraft that could take astronauts to the space station and beyond. Maybe there will even be a return trip to the moon, making the moon a station to launch more missions.

L is for looking up. The night sky is a show that is always changing. One of the ways to keep track of the stars is by finding pictures or constellations in the nighttime sky. Shapes in the stars—like a big pan called the Big Dipper—are easy to spot once you know how. It's just like a dot-to-dot picture in your coloring book.

L is for light, too. Stargazers will tell you that city lights can give off such a glow that it can spoil the sky show. For better viewing, it's often best to head with your family to the country, or to a beach or park, where you're not in the middle of the streetlights. Vacation is a good time to look at stars.

L is also for Leo the Lion, a favorite picture to spot in the stars. For help on finding Leo and other star pictures, head to a local planetarium. A planetarium is a domed theater that projects lights to form the stars and planets and shows their movements in the sky. A planetarium show will illustrate what you can see on the big sky screen in the night sky.

Check with local astronomy clubs, who sometimes organize star-watching parties.

Ll

L is for Looking up
to explore the amazing skies.
Astronomers give us charts and maps
to follow planets with our eyes.

Hercules

Corona
Borealis

Boötes

Alphecca

Arcturus

STAR CHART

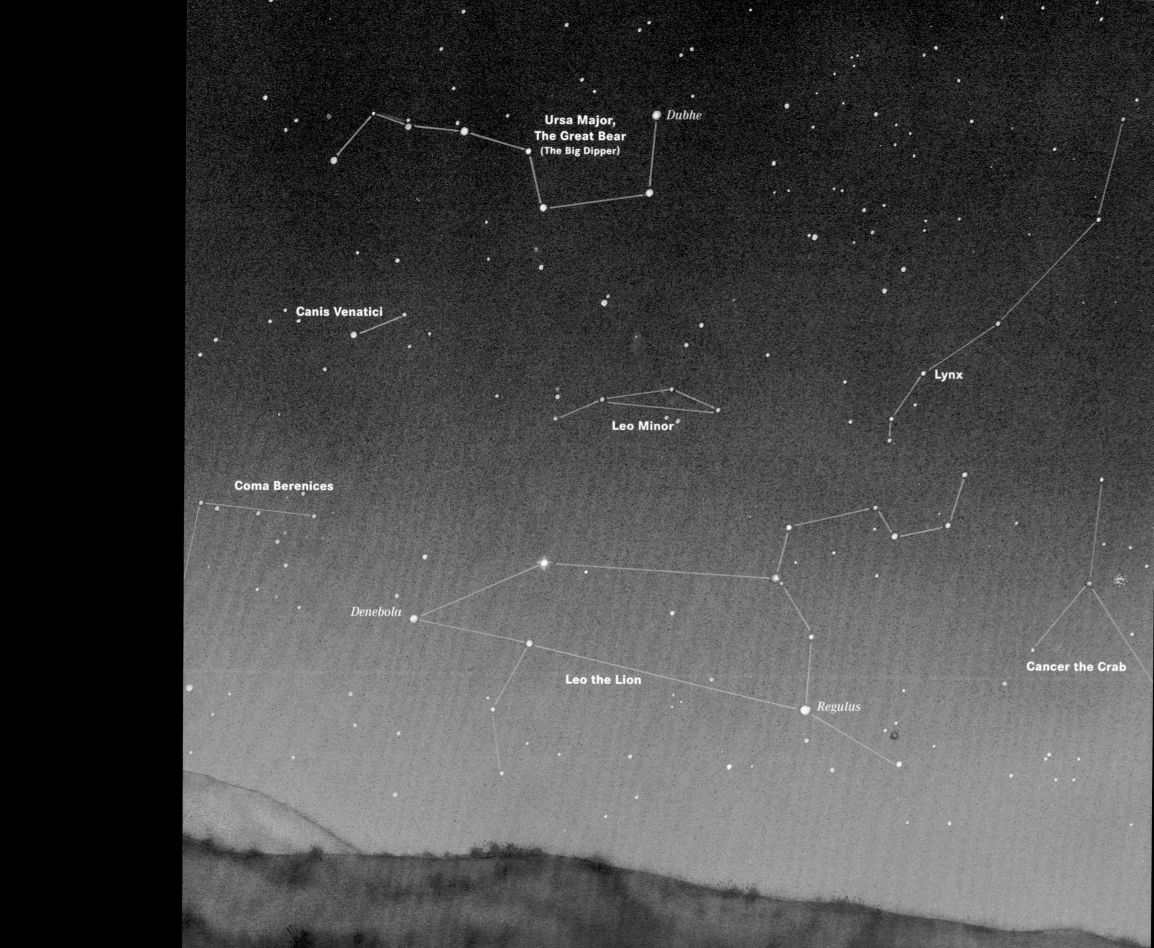

M is for Mercury,
  closest to the sun.
And for Mars,
  the only red one.

Mercury is the closet planet to the sun, but it's still about 36 million miles away from the sun. It's small and swift—one year on Mercury —the time it takes the planet to orbit around the sun—is only 88 days on Earth. The zippy little planet is named after the winged messenger god, Mercury, of the Romans. On Mercury, the temperatures are boiling hot in the daytime, about 800 degrees Fahrenheit. But the weather report for nights on Mercury is always the same: freezing cold, about—350 degrees Fahrenheit.

Mars is named after another Roman god, the god of war. It's also nicknamed the Red Planet, because of its color. We are learning more about the rocky red planet everyday as robots explore the land. It's more like Earth than other planets. It's the fourth planet from the sun and about half the size of Earth. A Martian day would be only half an hour longer than an Earth day. Could you live there? No, at least not right now. The air is too thin and the planet is too cold. But recent signs that Mars once had water has everyone excited to learn more about mysterious Mars.

M
m

N is for Neptune,
a planet full of gas and ice.
If you had to live there,
it wouldn't be so nice.

N
n

Neptune is named after the Roman god of the sea. Today, Neptune's icy-blue color reminds us of the sea. Neptune is the smallest of the family of gassy planets. There are four of them—Neptune, Jupiter, Saturn, and Uranus. Neptune is never likely to be a place astronauts will visit. Clouds of poisonous gases surround the planet. It's a frozen, cold place about 2.8 billion miles from the sun. Neptune wasn't discovered until 1846.

NASA is the name of the National Aeronautics and Space Administration—the people in charge of the United States program to explore space. In 1958 the group was formed by the U.S. government and got started working on the possibility of sending humans to explore space. The rest is history! NASA is now focusing on finishing work on the International Space Station and Mars exploration.

O is for the Orbit
of planets 'round the sun,
Mercury's path is shortest,
Neptune has the longest one.

Orbits are the paths the planets follow as they travel around the sun. An orbit is not like a highway with signs, but an invisible road. Don't worry; each planet knows its way.

The sun's gravity keeps each planet on its right path. Look at this page to see how the eight planets follow their own paths.

Pp

Saturn

Pluto
*(In 2006 Pluto became
a dwarf planet.)*

P is for Pluto—
a **dwarf** planet so small
that some people say
it's just like a tiny ice ball.

Until 2006 Pluto was classified as the ninth planet in our solar system. The International Astronomical Union, a worldwide group of astronomers, voted to reclassify Pluto from a planet to a new class, called dwarf planet.

Among the main reasons Pluto does not qualify as a true planet anymore is because its orbit crosses the orbital path of Neptune. Originally, scientists thought it was a much larger planet.

Most scientists agree with the new classification, and say it will lead to more exploration of the edge of the solar system where Pluto lies. This is an area called the Kuiper Belt. Look for more space news of other dwarf planets in the future.

This phrase below is a mnemonic, a phrase made up to help you remember a fact.

My	Very	Educated	Mother	Just
M**E**RCURY	V**E**NUS	**EARTH**	M**A**RS	J**U**PITER

Served	Us	Noodles
S**ATURN**	**URANUS**	**NEPTUNE**

Quiet? How quiet? You can make as much noise as you want in outer space and it won't bother anyone. Sound can't travel when there's no air so it's completely quiet in outer space.

Q is also for questions. The sky has always fascinated us. Asking questions and watching the sky is something people have done for hundreds and hundreds of years. Sometimes asking questions can get people in trouble. Polish astronomer Nicolaus Copernicus questioned the idea more than 450 years ago that the Earth was the center of everything. He figured out that the sun must be the center of our solar system. Later astronomers proved him right. The more we learn about our stars and planets, the more questions we have. What's your question?

Q is for Quiet.
There's no sound in outer space.
You couldn't hear your friend talking,
even if you were face to face.

R is for Robots
that help us out in space.
R is also for the rovers
that showed us Mars' red face.

Robots have been a huge help in exploring outer space. Robots can go where humans can't because they don't need to breathe, eat, or even sleep. The robot rovers on Mars are smart robots. In 2004 rovers named *Spirit* and *Opportunity* landed on Mars and began sending home amazing photos. NASA has big plans for robots in the future, especially to help us explore Mars. Robots will continue to be big helpers in future space exploration.

Rr

S s

S is for Saturn
and for the sun, too.
And for the stars to wish upon
that make our dreams come true.

Saturn is a beauty. Saturn is the sixth planet away from the sun and the second biggest planet. Named for the Roman god of harvest time, it is famous for its beautiful rings that surround the planet. The rings are made of ice, rock, and dust. This is a very cold planet since it's so far from the sun.

The sun, an enormous hot star, is the center of our solar system. Our solar system is made up of the planets, and everything that orbits around the sun, from big Jupiter to tiny moons. The sun is made up of gases and although not the biggest star or brightest, it is the closest, at 93 million miles away from Earth. The sun is what makes our life on Earth thrive and survive.

Have you ever wished on a star and said the rhyme, "Star light, star bright, the first star I see tonight, I wish I may, I wish I might, have the wish I wish tonight." People have been saying that rhyme for hundreds of years. It goes back to the belief that wishing on stars is lucky and can make a wish come true.

Thanks to the telescope, we are able to see the universe up close. Telescopes were used beginning in the early 1600s and changed the way we viewed the universe. A telescope makes objects appear brighter and clearer so we can see them better in the sky. There are many types of telescopes today that let scientists look at objects in space in different ways. Telescopes are powerful and important tools in the exploration of space.

Italian astronomer Galileo Galilei is believed to be the first to use a telescope to study the skies. He made many amazing discoveries. More recently, the powerful *Hubble* telescope orbiting around Earth sends back incredible pictures of planets, stars, and galaxies. The *Hubble* gets a visit about every three years from astronauts traveling on a space shuttle to repair anything that's broken. Hooray for the *Hubble*; it has opened up new windows on the worlds.

T t

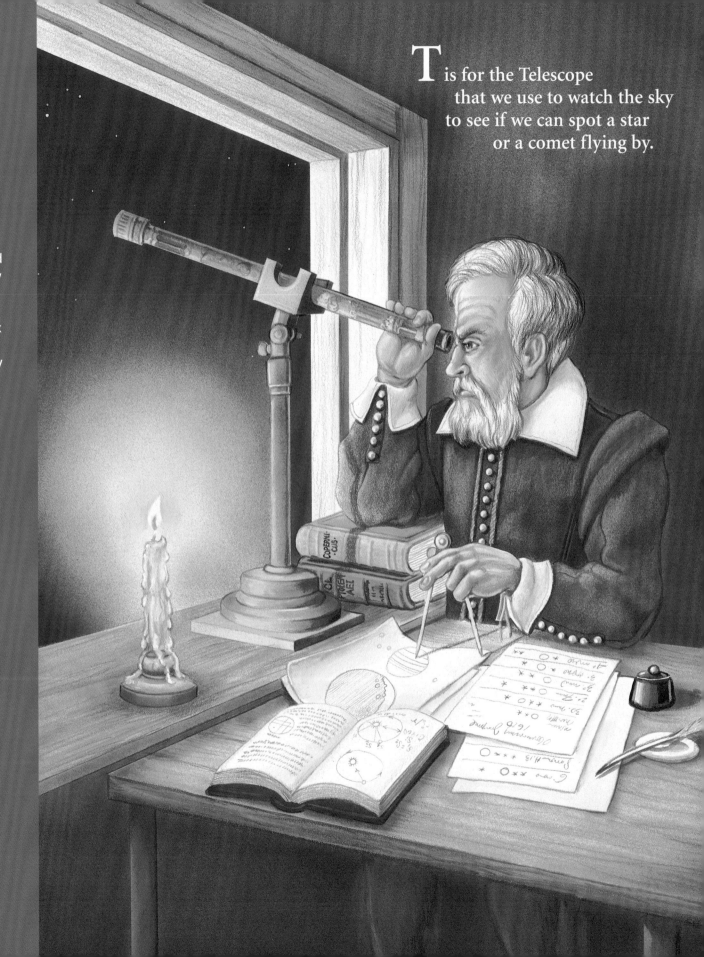

T is for the Telescope
   that we use to watch the sky
  to see if we can spot a star
    or a comet flying by.

U is for Uranus,
and for a Universe so unique,
where every star and planet
is one we want to seek.

You'll flip for Uranus, the planet on its side. Uranus is named after the Greek god of the sky. Uranus is the seventh planet away from the sun. As Uranus spins through the sky, it looks like a ball going through a hoop. Astronomers believe that a giant object at one time hit Uranus, tilting the planet on its side. Until Uranus was discovered in 1781 by William Herschel, people thought Saturn was on the edge of our solar system.

UFO stands for Unidentified Flying Object. Most scientists think that the UFOs can usually be explained as normal objects in space, including airplanes, comets, or shooting stars. Writers and moviemakers have had fun making UFOs come to life as alien spaceships.

Uu

V is for Venus,
a planet cloudy and hot,
with acid and poisonous gases,
it's quite an unlivable spot.

Venus is a bright beauty of a planet, but don't expect astronauts to visit.

Why? It's boiling hot; in fact it's hotter than boiling. Venus is hot enough that the surface is four times as hot as boiling water. Venus, named after the Roman goddess of love and beauty, wouldn't be livable for us. It is the second planet from the sun. The layer of thick clouds that adds to its beauty traps the heat in the planet so it can't escape. Scientists call this the greenhouse effect. You can see Venus at sunrise and sunset in certain times as the brightest star in the sky. Enjoy this planet from a distance.

We know that water is the key to life. Without it, we couldn't exist. Two-thirds of the Earth is covered by water. On Mars, signs of frozen water on the planet's surface have been shown in different space probes. Space watchers are excited that signs of water may lead to signs of life on the Red Planet. Who knows what kind of life scientists could discover?

When did women get to space? In 1963, Valentina Tereshkova became the first woman in space when she orbited around the earth in the *Vostok 6* mission for the former Soviet Union. Twenty years later, the first American woman Sally Ride flew into space aboard space shuttle *Challenger*. In 1992, Dr. Mae Jemison became the first African-American woman to orbit in space on the space shuttle *Endeavour*.

W is for Wondering.
Is there really life out there?
And W is for Water, too,
which we hope to find somewhere.

Have you ever heard of Planet X? It's not a real planet, but was the way astronomers talked about the existence of the possibility of finding another planet in the early 1900s. Astronomer Percival Lowell was sure there was another undiscovered planet, Planet X, and spent a lot of time searching for this planet. He never found one, but his apprentice Clyde Tombaugh believed he found one in 1930.

That discovery was named Pluto, which was classified as a planet until 2006. Pluto was reclassified as a dwarf planet.

Today's astronomers continue to learn more and find more objects in our universe. Who knows what they'll find in the future?

X is for Planet X,
   really just a name.
Finding another planet
   has been a tricky game.

Yy

Y is for Year—
the time it takes to go 'round the sun.
For every planet,
the measure is a different one.

Each year, you have a birthday and it takes a long time until you celebrate again. But if you lived on Jupiter, it would take 12 times as long to reach that birthday. A Jupiter year is equal to 12 Earth years. A year is the time it takes for a planet to orbit around the sun. Like birthday parties? Then you would like Mercury, where a year is only about 88 days.

Here's how the other planets measure up in Earth-years.

Mercury: 88 Earth days
Venus: 225 Earth days
Earth: 365 days
Mars: 687 days
Jupiter: 4,333 days (12 Earth years)
Saturn: 10,759 days (about 30 Earth years)
Uranus: 30,685 days (about 84 Earth years)
Neptune: 60,189 days (about 164 Earth years)

Sagittarius

Libra

Dschubba

Antares

Spica

Shaula

Virgo

Scorpio

Capricorn

Aquarius

Skat

Fomalhaut

Z is for Zodiac—
a name for 12 constellations.
The signs of the stars
have fascinated generations.

Algenib

Pisces

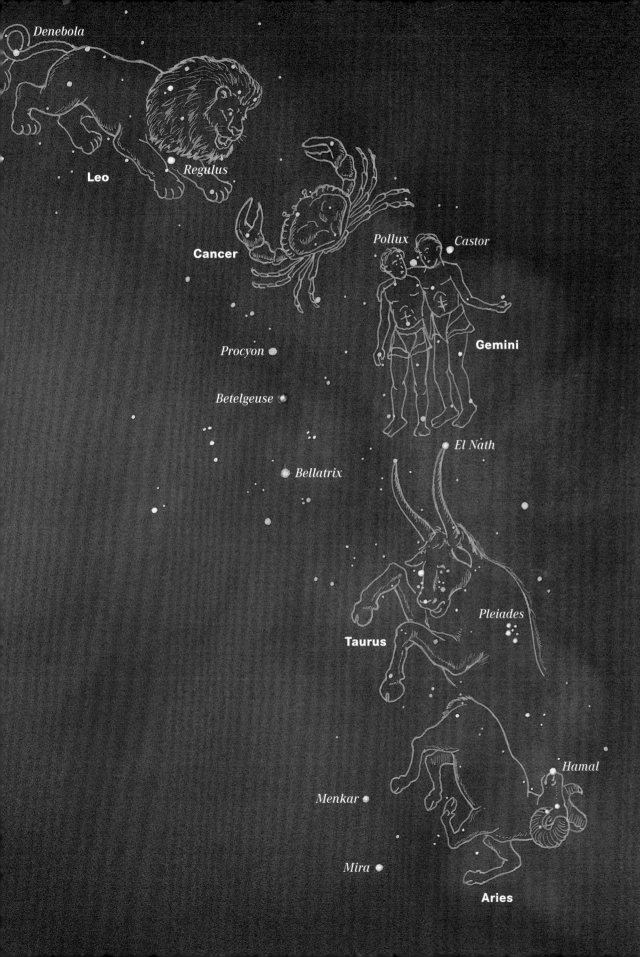

Denebola

Leo

Regulus

Cancer

Pollux *Castor*

Procyon

Gemini

Betelgeuse

Bellatrix

El Nath

Taurus

Pleiades

Hamal

Menkar

Mira

Aries

What's your sign? That's something people ask when they're talking about your zodiac sign. It all goes back to the Greeks, who saw animal patterns in the stars. They called the band of constellations the zodiac, or circle of animal signs. People used zodiac signs to tell fortunes and it is very popular. There's not any evidence that the stars affect your future, but many people enjoy reading horoscopes and keeping track of birth signs, or the constellations that were in the sky when you were born. Check your sign in the list below. Here are the dates that most horoscope watchers follow for identifying birthday signs.

Aries (*the ram*) March 21–April 19
Taurus (*the bull*) April 20–May 20
Gemini (*the twins*) May 21–June 20
Cancer (*the crab*) June 21–July 22
Leo (*the lion*) July 23–August 22
Virgo (*the virgin*) August 23–September 22
Libra (*the scales*) September 23–October 22
Scorpio (*the scorpion*) October 23–November 21
Sagittarius (*the archer*) November 22–December 21
Capricorn (*the goat*) December 22–January 19
Aquarius (*the water bearer*) January 20–February 18
Pisces (*the fish*) February 19–March 20

An Out of This World Quiz

1. Which planet is closest to the sun?

2. Which astronaut was the first American to step foot on the moon?

3. Most of the Earth's surface is covered with what?

4. What sentence is a good one to help you remember the order and names of the planets?

5. What former planet is now called a dwarf planet?

6. What is the name of the Roman god of the sea and a blue-looking planet?

7. Which president announced the goal of putting a man on the moon?

8. This astronomer predicted a comet would return. What is his name?

9. Who was the first American woman in space?

10. Which planet appears to be tilted on its side?

11. What planet is called the Red Planet?

12. What planet is not named after one of the gods or goddesses?

Answers

1. Mercury
2. Neil Armstrong
3. At least two-thirds of the Earth is covered with water.
4. My Very Educated Mother Just Served Us Noodles.
5. Pluto
6. Neptune
7. John F. Kennedy
8. Edmund Halley
9. Sally Ride
10. Uranus
11. Mars
12. Earth

End Note:

Fred Whipple, a Harvard University astronomer, is credited with creating the term
"dirty snowball" for a comet's nucleus.

Janis Campbell & Cathy Collison

Janis Campbell and Cathy Collison have been friends and writing partners for 10 years. They are interested in sharing information with young people on every topic under the sun, from stars in the news to the stars in the sky. They met at the *Detroit Free Press*, where they write and edit for "Yak's Corner," a magazine-style section for young readers.

Janis has interviewed astronaut Dr. Mae Jemison. A dozen years ago, Cathy found herself answering many questions about space in a *Detroit Free Press* column, "News for Young Readers." More recently, she visited NASA's Kennedy Space Center for a story on the return to flight.

They have collaborated on several books, including *Authors by Request*, a book profiling 12 hot authors for young readers. Both live in Michigan and are married, with two children each. This is their first book with Sleeping Bear Press.

Alan Stacy

Alan created his first painting at the age of 18 months—on a wall at home! Luckily, his mother—also an artist—encouraged him from the start, enrolling him in an adult drawing class at the age of eight. Alan's father, an Air Force pilot, took the family to Germany, Virginia, Alaska, and New Mexico before settling in Texas in 1975. Alan credits his family's travels for his profound love of animals and nature, which is reflected in his art.

Alan worked in broadcast television as a graphic artist for many years before becoming a self-employed illustrator and designer. Alan also teaches cartooning, comic book art, and illustration. He is also the illustrator for *L is for Lone Star: A Texas Alphabet* and *Round Up: A Texas Number Book*. He lives in Arlington, Texas.

Alan's dad was part of the team that chose the astronauts for the *Gemini* and early *Apollo* space programs in the early 1960s.